W9-ANA-781

FROM THE
Library of

Clara Crenshaw

ONE THOUSAND MOONS

KRISHNAMURTI AT EIGHTY-FIVE

Krishnamurti in India, 1980.

TEXT AND PHOTOGRAPHS BY ASIT CHANDMAL

ONE THOUSAND MOONS

KRISHNAMURTI AT EIGHTY-FIVE

HARRY N. ABRAMS, INC., PUBLISHERS, NEW YORK

AUTHOR'S NOTE
I have made no attempt to either summarize or expound Krishnamurti's
teachings; for that one must go to the man, to his talks, and to his
books. However, I have included in my memoirs of Krishnamurti incidents
and conversations that I believe convey something worth
preserving: how Krishnamurti talks to and counsels a child, a young
man, and a middle-aged worldly adult. At every age, whenever I had
a problem, I went to Krishnamurti. I received great affection and
advice that solved my problem for at least a short time.
Much had to be left out; one has to read between the lines.
In some places throughout the text, I have referred to Krishnamurti as Krishnaji, the latter a name people call him in India.
A. C.

Editor: Anne Yarowsky
Designer: Tina Davis Snyder

Library of Congress Cataloging in Publication Data

Chandmal, Asit.
One thousand moons.

1. Krishnamurti, J. (Jiddu), 1895-
2. Philosophers—India—Biography. I. Title.
II. Title: 1000 moons.
B5134.K754C48 1985   181'.4   84-29780
ISBN 0-8109-1209-0

Copyright © 1985 Asit Chandmal

Published in 1985 by Harry N. Abrams, Incorporated, New York.
All rights reserved. No part of the contents of this book may be
reproduced without the written permission of the publishers

Printed and bound in Japan

CONTENTS

Krishnamurti, 1934. Photo by Edward Weston.

© 1981 Center for Creative Photography, Arizona Board of Regents.

PREFACE

The idea for this book came while I was with Krishnamurti in Madras in January 1980. It occurred to me that there was no dichotomy between his life and his teachings. The teachings were intellectual, logical, and rigorous. His daily life and conversations were simple. He was an ordinary human being in private life, and yet the other Krishnamurti, the teacher, was clearly of extraordinary energy, intelligence, and insight. The man on the public platform and the man away from it were different, but there was no contradiction between what he said and what he did.

I used to wonder why the words of a Buddha or a Christ or a Mohammed could still capture the minds and hearts of more than half of humanity. These were simple men, who lived millennia ago, and yet their powerful hold on so many people was beyond all understanding when one considered the thinkers who had preceded and followed them. What did these men have or do that others did not?

And so I turned to Krishnamurti. His life was a legend. I knew him well. If I could spend time traveling with him, being with him, photographing him, observing how he actually lived, then perhaps I could find an answer. I asked Krishnamurti if I could do a book on him. He agreed readily. He said I could do what I wanted, take photographs at any time, in any situation, and write about whatever I saw and felt.

And so the book began, with the first tentative, hesitant photographs. As I traveled with him, and watched him, I found that there was nothing he forbade me. I took pictures, I started writing. And then a strange thing happened. Instead of his life unfolding, I found that the more I probed the more I came face to face with myself. As I explored his life, his quotidian activities, I began to confront myself more and more, to reexamine everything about my own daily life. In the beginning it was effortless; there was a recollection of my conversations with him at various times since I was nine years old. Later it became more difficult, as if I wanted to erase the responses excavated by his questions.

So what began as a journey into another man's life ended with an unfinished journey into mine.

I did not find the answer to my original question. Perhaps the immense energy that comes into being when there is no conflict between what you think, what you say, and what you do, results in direct communication, which is independent of time, and therefore exists for many generations.

This book was conceived and created in Krishnaji's eighty-fifth year; he had lived for a thousand months, or a thousand moons, hence the title.

The book is dedicated to my grandmother, Iravati Mehta, or Moti Mama as we all called her. My grandmother told me when I was nine, "It is more important to be with Krishnaji than to go to school," and she acted accordingly and took me with her to Poona to stay with Krishnaji. I did not have the same insight or courage when it came to my own children, Clea and Sonali, but in the making of this book, falteringly, hesitantly, I started moving toward the same conclusion. Perhaps it is too late.

My aunts, Pupul Jayakar, the most intelligent, and Nandini Mehta, the most beautiful, had their lives altered totally, but in different ways, by their meetings with Krishnaji. They have their own stories to tell, and they will be told in Pupul Jayakar's forthcoming book on Krishnaji. The chapter in this book on his daily life at eighty-five has been extracted, with modifications, from the draft manuscript of Pupul Jayakar's book.

A great many people assisted in the compilation of this book. Mary Zimbalist was supportive and instructive from the start. Mary Lutyens and Mary Cadogan offered the help I asked for; Paul Gottlieb, the publisher, was quick and decisive, and later very patient with me and sensitive to the needs of publishing the kind of book that his company, Harry N. Abrams, does not normally publish. Tina Davis worked heroically to sort through almost fifteen hundred photographs, all uncaptioned; she was in New York, and I in either Asia or Europe. We met once in New York to finalize the layouts—she had done an excellent job in decoding the photos and instinctively recognizing the documentary importance of some of them. Incidentally all photographs were taken in available light and not one was arranged or posed. The idea was to document and record, not to take beautiful pictures. Charan and Nimisha Sharma, and my wife, Minakshi, did the first layout and dummy that I showed to Paul Gottlieb. These fifteen hundred photographs of Krishnaji are like family snapshots to me—I find every one of them worth keeping and impossible to discard. Without Nimisha, Charan, Minakshi, and Tina, the photographs would have remained unsorted and unedited. The final version was compiled by Anne Yarowsky.

This book owes its existence to M, who helped so much.

Krishnamurti in Adyar, 1910.

KRISHNAMURTI:
HIS EARLY LIFE

Madanapalle is a small town in the heart of South India. It is in the Chittoor District of Andhra Pradesh, about 150 miles from Madras.

A century ago a young Brahmin named Jiddu Narianiah moved to Madanapalle with his wife, Jiddu Sanjeevamma, who was also his second cousin. (The family name, Jiddu, came from their ancestral village.)

Like others of his caste, Narianiah had a puja room in his home. Puja is prayer. An orthodox Brahmin woman does not enter the puja room or a temple while giving birth. It is sacrilegious.

Sanjeevamma insisted on giving birth to her eighth child in the puja room.

The child was born half an hour after midnight on May 11, 1895, or 12:30 A.M. on May 12. He was named Krishnamurti, after Lord Krishna, who was also the eighth born according to Hindu mythology.

It is recorded that Krishnamurti's horoscope was cast by the local astrologer, who predicted religious greatness and global fame for the infant.

Until he was almost fifteen, nothing in the boy's life gave any indication that he would be famous; nothing in his behavior for the next twenty years, till he was almost thirty-five, gave any indication that he would be a great religious teacher. And yet this was the man about whom the greatest skeptics in the world, who were also the most articulate of men, wrote in terms that had the dimension of hyperbole.

George Bernard Shaw called Krishnamurti "a religious figure of the greatest distinction," and added, "He is the most beautiful human being I have ever seen."

Henry Miller wrote, "There is no man I would consider it a greater privilege to meet...."

Aldous Huxley, after attending one of Krishnamurti's lectures, confided in a letter "...the most impressive thing I have listened to. It was like listening to a discourse of the Buddha—such power, such intrinsic authority...."

Kahlil Gibran wrote, "When he entered my room I said to myself, 'Surely the Lord of Love has come.'"

•

Krishnamurti, at ninety, is still very much alive. He travels the world, addresses thousands in the United States, Asia, and Europe; is interviewed, televised, published, feted, adored, worshiped, and criticized; and yet his life is an enigma. While every detail of his early years has been meticulously recorded, it is full of myth, magic, and mystery. When you meet Krishnamurti, and are mesmerized by his magic, your modern mind starts believing the legends of his youth. The mystery, however, remains.

Krishnamurti hides nothing. He has seminars and dialogues with world-famous scientists, writers, psychiatrists, artists, sociologists, Buddhist scholars, politicians and prime ministers, and yet the mystery remains.

And so instead of attempting to interpret or understand or explain his life, one can merely repeat what others have witnessed and recorded.

•

The story begins even earlier than 1895. The Theosophical Society was founded in 1875 in New York City by Madame Helena Petrovna Blavatsky, née Von Hahn. She was of Russian origin and had based the principles of the Society on many esoteric and occult teachings—the Kabala, Gnosticism, Meister Eckhart, Paracelsus, and later, Hindu, Buddhist, and Tibetan beliefs such as karma and reincarnation.

However, two central beliefs are important and relevant to any retelling of the life of Krishnamurti. The first, that there are Masters, or Adepts, who are perfected human beings and who guide the spiritual evolution of Man. Some of these Masters live in the Himalayas and can be contacted on the astral plane by those who have the occult powers to do so.

The second belief is that Lord Maitreya (who in the Theosophical hierarchy is even higher than the Masters but lower than the Buddha) would again reincarnate himself in a human body, as he had done in the body of Jesus.

The coming of the World Teacher was therefore central to Theosophy; it would happen when Lord Maitreya found the right body, the right vehicle, to incarnate in, and the body, the being, would be prepared and protected by the Masters. None of this, by itself, would be astonishing. However, Madame Blavatsky, and later Dr. Annie Besant, actually set up a worldwide organization to prepare for the coming of the World Teacher.

One of the organization's purposes was to "find" a person, somewhere on earth, whose being and body were such that the Lord Maitreya himself could incarnate in the found vehicle. And the only thing the leaders of the Society had to go on was their faith in their own occult powers.

Annie Besant, née Wood, was born in 1847 in London. She

read Madame Blavatsky's book *The Secret Doctrine* when she was about forty. She was immediately converted. She met Blavatsky in 1888 and joined the Theosophical Society in 1889.

Annie Besant would have been considered a remarkable woman in any society, in any era. She separated from her husband when she was twenty-six and plunged into the most modern causes and movements. She was a close associate of Charles Bradlaugh, a great public figure and atheist; she advocated birth control publicly and vigorously; she became a prominent Fabian, counting George Bernard Shaw and Sidney and Beatrice Webb among her close friends and colleagues; she was president of the Theosophical Society from 1907 until her death in 1933; and in 1916 she founded the Indian Home Rule League, striving with figures such as Mahatma Gandhi for Indian independence; and she was considered one of the greatest orators of her time.

It was she who would "adopt" the boy Krishnamurti, proclaim him the coming Messiah, the World Teacher to be, set up an enormous global organization with large funds and thousands of followers to provide the infrastructure for Krishnamurti's teachings, take great personal interest in his upbringing and education (Krishnamurti always called her Amma or Mother), and remain utterly loyal to Krishnamurti even when he rejected the great organization she had built for him.

But Krishnamurti was "found" by another man – Charles Webster Leadbeater, who had journeyed in 1884 with Blavatsky to India, to Adyar, Madras, where she had set up the Theosophical Society headquarters. Leadbeater was a powerful figure, resembling George Bernard Shaw, and he claimed to have developed occult powers, including the ability to see and interpret the aura surrounding each human being; he also claimed to be able to communicate with the Masters.

Narianiah retired and moved to Adyar in January 1909. Krishnamurti's mother had died four years earlier, and Narianiah's family consisted of his four surviving sons.

Krishnamurti was the second eldest of the four and had spent his childhood as a dreamy and vague boy, not interested in school or learning, but fascinated by nature and mechanical things. He would watch ants for hours or take apart his father's watch to see how it worked. He was attached to his mother and to his younger brother, Nitya, but evidently to nothing else, especially not to any material things. He was regularly punished at school, but it did not seem to have any effect on him. This was a quality that he has retained throughout his life: neither praise nor criticism leaves a mark on him. Equally, no one else's thoughts or ideas have ever influenced him, a quality that stood him in good stead when he was being brought up and educated by Theosophists in the East and the West. Krishnamurti once described this as being like a vessel with many holes: whatever is poured in goes out, nothing remains.

It was 1909, and Krishnamurti was fourteen years old. He was playing and bathing on the beach at Adyar. Leadbeater saw Krishnamurti's aura and found it wonderful, with not a particle of selfishness in it. It was suggested to Narianiah that the Theosophical Society would bring up Krishnamurti and his younger brother, Nitya. And so began the grooming of the World Teacher. The discovery of Krishnamurti is inexplicable unless you are a believer in Leadbeater's occult powers.

Krishnamurti was "instructed" by the Masters, especially Master Kuthumi, who was fair, with blue eyes, brown hair and beard, and lived somewhere in Tibet in the body of his last incarnation, that of a Kashmiri Brahmin. With the help of Leadbeater, Krishnamurti would visit the Master Kuthumi on the astral plane at night and write down his teachings in the morning. His writings were eventually published in 1910, when Krishnamurti was fifteen. Titled *At the Feet of the Master*, it has been translated into almost thirty languages, and it is still in print. During the day Leadbeater and his close associates gave Krishnamurti a more conventional education. They taught him English, not only the language but modes of behavior.

The boy had undoubted psychic powers that were revealed when they tested him. He could easily read unopened letters and people's thoughts.

In 1911, Annie Besant took Krishnamurti and his brother Nitya to England. They returned to India for a short visit and in 1912 went back to England. They were to stay in Europe for ten years before seeing India again.

The boys were brought up in aristocratic upper-class English society, primarily by Lady Emily Lutyens, the daughter of a viceroy of India and the wife of Sir Charles Lutyens, the architect of New Delhi. They did all the normal things for boys of their age and situation in society — had private tutors, dressed immaculately, cultivated beautiful manners, spoke English and French perfectly, went to the theater, played golf, and vacationed on the Continent. Slowly every vestige of his Hindu boyhood was removed from Krishnamurti.

Krishnamurti proceeded to fail every single examination he sat for. He was refused admission to Oxford despite his connections (one of them purportedly being the son of God), and he could not complete his studies at London University or at the Sorbonne.

Krishnamurti was probably an unhappy, agitated, and lonely boy, who seems to have undergone some of the afflictions of adolescence. Mrs. Besant was too busy fighting for freedom in India, and Krishnamurti and Nitya were virtually living in exile during the First World War in an alien country. Krishnamurti was constantly being reminded that he had a great future, great responsibilities, for he would be the World Teacher, and thousands in many countries were donating money and devoting their lives to building an organization for him and his teachings, and many more thousands were eagerly awaiting the day when he would appear before them and propound the Teachings.

One of the tangibles in Krishnamurti's life is that none of this seems to have had any effect on him inwardly. Outwardly, he was, and has remained, a shy, considerate, and gentle person;

however he seems to have been vague and even frivolous in those days, qualities difficult to imagine for anyone who has come across him in the last fifty years. Mrs. Besant, Leadbeater, and the Theosophists really protected Krishnamurti. Nobody could touch him or, even, his tennis racket. As far as possible he had two companions, and even the adjoining compartments of the train in which he traveled were occupied by his protectors.

His brother Nitya had been given the same upbringing, but he did not have to become the World Teacher. Nitya and Krishnamurti were devoted to each other. Nitya was bright and passed his exams easily. He wanted to make money, marry, and live a normal life. All this was denied to him. He was to protect and look after Krishnamurti. Nitya was never very healthy physically and was to contract tuberculosis.

It was suggested to Krishnamurti that the climate at Ojai, a valley inland from Santa Barbara, California, would be ideal for Nitya. The American Indians called the valley Ojai, or the nest, and it is covered with groves of orange trees. Krishnamurti and Nitya went to Ojai and stayed in a place called Pine Cottage.

It was here, in August 1922, that a strange "process" began, the first external evidence that something inexplicable and mystical was happening to Krishnamurti. There were several eye-witnesses, and Nitya wrote an account of the process for Mrs. Besant and Charles Leadbeater. Krishnamurti too wrote about his experiences.

For three days, from August 17 through August 20, Krishnamurti's body was racked with pain. He was unconscious a great deal of the time, cried out, could not bear to be touched, complained of dirty surroundings and pain in his head and neck, fainted, did not eat, shivered and yet complained of heat, was in agony most of the time and strangely quiet for some of the time, and then on the third day he sat under a young pepper tree and started chanting. The Buddha, Lord Maitreya, and other celestial beings seem to have appeared before Krishnamurti, and he went into a deep trance. Krishnamurti's account of this experience ends with the words "I am God intoxicated."

Neither Annie Besant nor Charles Leadbeater could fully explain this process, which Krishnamurti was to undergo with some variations at different times for many years.

One explanation was that his brain and body were being purified to the nth degree so that the Lord Maitreya could inhabit the vehicle. Another explanation is that it was the rising of the Kundalini in Krishnamurti's body; the Kundalini and its awakening, from the base of the spine, upward along the spine and neck to the centers of the brain and the opening of the third eye, has been described for millennia by Hindu sages. The descriptions are uncannily similar to Krishnamurti's experiences.

Krishnamurti has no memory now of his experiences of the

Krishnamurti with Nitya, 1910.

Krishnamurti in India, 1948.

process. Knowing the absolute integrity and total lack of superstitious mumbo jumbo in Krishnamurti, one can only state that something vitally important and completely inexplicable happened to Krishnamurti in August 1922, when he was twenty-seven years old.

Outwardly his life did not change. He continued to travel, to give talks organized under the auspices of the Theosophical Society, and the Order of the Star of the East, which had been created for him. And he did not say anything startling or different. He seemed a follower, a person being prepared to be a vehicle for the World Teacher.

In 1923 Annie Besant bought Pine Cottage and six acres in Ojai for Krishnamurti and Nitya; the land had a larger house that was renamed Arya Vihar and was next to Pine Cottage and the pepper tree. Several hundred acres of land were later bought for future use, for starting schools.

Baron von Pallandt offered Castle Eerde, in Ommen, Holland, with five thousand acres of land to Krishnamurti; this was used to hold annual "camps" or conventions.

And then the great turning point in Krishnamurti's life occurred in November 1925.

Krishnamurti and Nitya were at Ojai, and Nitya had not been well. Krishnamurti was asked to travel to India to give talks organized by the Theosophical Society. He did not want to leave Nitya alone. However he was assured by the leaders of the Society that the Masters would protect Nitya. Nitya would not be allowed to die.

Reluctantly Krishnamurti left for India. When his ship was in the Suez Canal he received a telegram: Nitya had died.

Krishnamurti was stunned. According to eyewitnesses, who were also close associates, Krishnamurti wept for several days and nights. However he stayed with his sorrow, making no attempt at escape or explanation, and by the time the ship reached India, the crisis had passed.

But Krishnamurti was never to depend on anything or be attached to anyone again, and this became a central theme in his teachings.

From 1926 to 1929 Krishnamurti continued traveling to India, Europe, and America. However a change had clearly taken place, evident from his pronouncements at various public gatherings. He had become more thoughtful, more serious, less willing to be told what to do.

The great break with the Theosophical Society came in August 1929. At the Ommen Camp in Holland, in front of Mrs. Besant and an audience of more than three thousand members, Krishnamurti dissolved the Order of the Star. Among other things, he said that Truth was a pathless land, and no organization should be formed to lead or coerce people along any particular path, because Truth, being limitless and unconditional, could not be organized and was unapproachable through any religion, sect, or organization.

He said he did not want to belong to any organization of a spiritual kind, because such an organization becomes a crutch, a weakness, a bondage, and cripples the individual.

He said that he did not want any followers or disciples, because the moment you follow someone you cease to follow Truth.

He said that no one holds the key to Truth, that key is your own self, and in the purification and incorruptibility of that self alone...

He said that he had contemplated the situation for over two years, slowly, carefully, and patiently; that he had not been persuaded by anyone ("I am not persuaded in such things") and that his decision was final.

It was a great shock to everyone. Krishnamurti resigned from the Theosophical Society and from every organization, Order, and Trust of which he was a member. He gave up everything that had been given to him.

He was thirty-four years old.

Krishnamurti had never had any desire for money, power, or a comfortable life. When people told him that his was a magnificent act of renunciation and asked him what he would now do, Krishnamurti replied that his only concern was to set man free, to free man from all cages, from all fears; he would not found a new religion nor establish new theories or philosophies. Instead he would go around the world, meeting and talking to people, because "if there are only five people who will listen, who will live, who have their faces turned to eternity, it will be sufficient."

Annie Besant remained loyal to him. She died in 1933, at eighty-six, and Charles Leadbeater died in 1934 at the age of eighty-seven.

Krishnamurti spent the years of the Second World War at Ojai. It was during those years that he met and befriended Aldous Huxley and other intellectuals. He moved equally easily with their friends from Hollywood, among whom were Greta Garbo, Charlie Chaplin, and John Barrymore. (He turned down the latter's offer to act as the Buddha in a film. He was to be paid five thousand dollars a week.)

He went to India in 1948, a time of great upheaval. India had just become independent, and when Mahatma Gandhi was assassinated, it has been written that "it was to Krishnamurti that Jawaharlal Nehru brought, in secret, his solitary anguish."

Huxley encouraged Krishnamurti to write and to publish. *Education and the Significance of Life* (1953), *The First and Last Freedom* (1954), and *Commentaries on Living* (1956) became the first of over thirty books published through the years in the United States, Europe, and India. They are written in his own words, and together with his public talks—many of which are available on videocassettes—they contain his teachings as they unfolded in the last four decades.

It is impossible to summarize Krishnamurti's teachings. I am convinced that the printed words by themselves do not convey as much as the public talks do, and that the public talks take on much greater meaning when one sees the teachings personified in the daily life of Krishnamurti.

KRISHNAMURTI'S LIFE
AT AGE EIGHTY-FIVE

Krishnaji wakes at sunrise, and lies in bed, every sense alert. Not a single thought arises, and then there is a coming to, from vast distances.

He starts the morning with forty-five minutes of yogic asanas and thirty-five minutes of pranayam, or breathing exercises.

At about eight, Krishnaji has breakfast, which consists of fruit; cereal such as muesli; yogurt; nuts; eggs; toast; and butter—never tea or coffee. His breakfast in India sometimes includes South Indian idlis or dosas instead of cereal. He drinks a tablespoon of the green juice of a bitter gourd.

In the West he breakfasts alone and quietly. In India, however, his close associates gather. Over breakfast there is discussion on education and the schools, on consciousness, the seed of disintegration in man, computers and artificial intelligence, the possible mutation of the human mind, on death, the nature of God, and so on.

The conversation moves to international affairs, scientific discoveries, war and nuclear disarmament. Krishnaji has an intense curiosity and questions deeply. New discoveries in science and new technological advances fascinate him.

He asks for news of what is happening in the world. The state of the country is freely discussed; the violence, corruption, the decay of values; every problem is raised and probed.

Everyone participates, and there is no sense of the teacher and the taught.

There are questions he often asks: What is happening in the country? Why has it lost all creativity? Why is there degeneration? No one answer satisfies him. It is as if the serious individual has to hold these questions within him to awaken to their intimations. The questions have to be asked and the mind remain with them, ponder them. Krishnaji's span of attention is formidable. He once said that some questions have to be held in the mind for eternity.

When he is to hold his morning dialogues, the breakfast session is shorter. A small group that is to participate in the discussions gathers at ten and the discussions continue until eleven-thirty. When there are no organized group discussions, his talks with his associates continue at the breakfast table for two or three hours. Some of his most intense insights have been revealed at these sessions. He often refers to himself in the third person—as "K"—during these conversations.

By eleven-thirty he goes to his room and lies down for half an hour with the *Economist, Time,* or *Newsweek;* or picture books of trees, mountains, birds, and animals; or detective and mystery novels. He never reads serious books, but is very well informed on the state of the world.

At midday, he has an oil massage, a very hot bath, and lunch is at one-fifteen.

Krishnaji eats very slowly; his associates finish eating long before he does. He tastes and chews everything very carefully and savors and comments on the food when it's excellent. Lunch usually lasts over two hours.

In India he eats Indian food, though he always starts with fruit and salad. He rarely eats fried or sweet food. He likes hot pickles and permits himself tiny portions of them. Again at lunchtime there is discussion. In the West he first eats fruit and salads, in that order, then soup, followed by a cooked dish, which could be Italian, French, Mexican, or English. It is at lunch that discussions with his friends and associates take place in the West. Krishnaji sometimes tells stories, talks about his encounters with wild animals, or jokes about St. Peter, heaven and hell, as well as stories of Russia and the commissars. He intersperses these with serious talk.

In the West Krishnaji helps to clear the table, wash the dishes, and clean the kitchen. In India, the servants take care of that. After lunch he returns to his room and takes a nap. At about four o'clock, he sees a few people: a woman going blind or a mother grieving over the death of her child.

With the sun about to set, he goes for a walk. His strides are long, his body erect. His friends walk with him. He walks briskly for five kilometers, watching, listening, smelling the earth. He picks up and throws aside stones lying on the path. There is very little conversation. He has said that not a single thought touches his mind during these walks.

He hardly ever misses his walk, regardless of the weather or how he is feeling. On a long flight I have seen him walk up and down the aisle of the plane.

Returning home, he washes, then once again does some breathing exercises. He eats a light supper—the food is the same as at lunch. On some occasions, with a few friends, he sits over the dinner table and hints of an eternity that lies beyond the mind. In the West, he eats alone in bed, his food on a tray, while watching television or reading a book.

When he is not feeling well, or to keep himself physically healthy, he tries all kinds of herbal and ayurvedic remedies. He regularly takes vitamin and mineral tablets with breakfast. He experiments with his diet; at times he has gone on a protein diet; at times he has drunk a sip of milk and orange juice alternately; at other times he has given up all milk and lived on raw foods. For the past twenty years he has insisted on eating fruit first, then raw salads, and only then cooked food, with a little dessert at the end. He does not drink wine or any other alcoholic beverage and has never smoked in his life. He has always been a vegetarian.

He is very particular about his clothes and looks after them carefully. He is always elegantly and appropriately dressed—whether it be jeans, shirt, and jogging shoes in California, or a suit in London, or Indian clothes in India. He likes to polish his own shoes and sometimes those of others.

He occasionally goes to see movies: he likes Westerns. He sometimes visits museums. He watches television very often and listens to classical music, both Western and Indian.

Every year Krishnamurti travels throughout the world talking to individuals, small groups, or addressing thousands of people at public talks. He has been traveling for over sixty years, never staying more than a few weeks in each place. He has traveled and spoken directly to more people than any man in history.

He only goes where he is invited. From mid-February to the end of May, he is in the United States, mainly in Ojai, California, eighty miles north of Los Angeles. He stays at Pine Cottage near Arya Vihar. He has lived there since 1922. He gives several public talks. He makes trips to New York, San Francisco, or, say, Los Alamos, New Mexico, if invited to give talks or hold seminars. There is a Krishnamurti Foundation of America (KFA) school at Ojai where he talks to the parents and staff about education and the significance of life.

He spends June at the KFE school in Brockwood Park, Hampshire, England. The school was founded in 1969 with a large part of the initial money funded by a gift the donor originally intended to give to Krishnamurti for his personal use. At Brockwood he has discussions with the teachers, students, and staff.

He moves to Gstaad, Switzerland, in July. A chalet is rented. Krishnamurti eats at the chalet, occasionally driving to a restaurant for lunch. Krishnamurti holds several question-and-answer sessions, and gives six or seven public talks to about three thousand people who come to hear him every year. He returns to Brockwood Park in the second half of August and stays until the end of October. Again there are several public talks and discussions, as well as private interviews.

Starting in November he spends three and a half months in India. He goes to New Delhi first and then Benares, where he stays on the grounds of the educational institutions founded by him at Rajghat over the last fifty years. He spends about two or three weeks in each place.

He then moves to Madras, where he stays at Vasant Vihar, the headquarters of the KFI. He spends four weeks in Madras, and then three to four weeks at the school in Rishi Valley, a hundred and fifty miles east of Madras, which he founded in 1926.

On his way to Europe and the United States, he spends three weeks in Bombay, and lives in the Sterling Apartments.

At his public talks in India, some of which are attended by about seven thousand people, he still wears a broad red-bordered dhoti and a long honey-toned kurta. In the West, he wears a shirt, slacks, and a cardigan, or a suit if he talks in a city. Krishnamurti walks to the dais surrounded—but untouched—by people. As he sits in silence on the platform, Krishnamurti's presence reaches out and draws his listeners close to him. Then he starts to speak.

The back is erect, the face untouched by time. The voice is clear, strong, probing, unfolding the problem, letting it open and reveal itself, exploring every nuance. His hands rest in his lap, occasionally they move, gesturing eloquently. For over an hour and a half the vast audience sits, silent, with hardly any movement. After the talk is over Krishnamurti sits still.

The thousands in the audience sit or stand motionless as if totally absorbed.

In Switzerland, Krishnamurti walks out of the tent after his talk, onto a path leading toward Saanen. He walks briskly. Men, women, and children come out of the tent and gaze at him, standing still as if mesmerized. After a couple of hundred yards he gets into the car that takes him back to the chalet.

In England, Krishnamurti returns, after changing his clothes, to the tent where lunch is served. Krishnamurti mixes with the audience. Everyone is polite. No one stares at him. Someone comes up and engages him in some inconsequential conversation. Krishnamurti eats standing up or walking around.

In India, he folds his hands in namaste and the crowds surge toward him. He reaches out with both hands and allows them to be held by those that can reach him. Then, slowly, he extricates himself. He gets down from the platform. There is only a tiny passage through this mass of people. They touch their faces to his hands. He does not draw his hands away but keeps them extended. It looks as if a stampede is inevitable, but the silence of his presence creates order. People move back slightly and he walks through.

In Bombay, in the car, when his companions try to close the window, Krishnamurti stops them. His arms reach out through the windows. All the way to the gate, men and women press on the car, touching his hands, putting them to their eyes. Children wait at the Sterling Apartments flat with a garland of jasmine and roses. He takes it with grace, wears it around his neck for some moments, before giving it to a child near him. He does not like people to touch his feet, bending to touch theirs if they attempt to.

As he enters his tenth decade, the urgency has increased, so has the drive. Nothing seems to tire him. He pushes the body, walking faster, testing himself, so that most people half his age cannot keep up with him.

By ten-thirty at night he is asleep. Just before he sleeps the whole day passes swiftly through his mind. In a flash the day and its events are quenched. He rarely dreams. There are no yesterdays.

In 1980, Krishnamurti was to tell my aunt, Pupul Jayakar, that when he stopped speaking, his body would die. The body existed for only one purpose, to reveal the Teaching.

KRISHNAMURTI: A MEMOIR

When I was nine I stayed with Krishnaji in Poona for several weeks. My grandmother had set up house in the Servants of India Society—there were two bedrooms and a living room in between. The dining room and the kitchen were in a separate cottage two hundred yards away.

We used to walk together to the cottage for lunch—his umbrella always protecting him against even a hint of sun.

He often asked me to run to the cottage—he ran with me, and we finished together. I was nine and he was six times my age—fifty-four.

When he saw me flying kites he told me about the enormous kites in California, larger in span than his outstretched arms, and later, when it was Diwali, we went to the markets of Poona, bought firecrackers, and lit them at night. Once, when I shied away from a bursting bomb he said, "Watch it. Don't look away."

•

When I was fourteen, I visited him at Ratansi Morarji's house on Carmichael Road in Bombay.

I asked him, "Should I meditate?"

He said, "No, you are too young. Play with it. Play with everything. Look at girls, flowers. Don't take things seriously. The mind does not mature until it is forty."

The next day I went to see him again at Carmichael Road. We sat quietly. I felt a gradual untangling of myself, and as it evolved, I could sense resistance, reluctance to let go. Pure peace flooded me. (I am trying to revive a memory that has committed suicide.) After a few minutes I left. We had not spoken, not touched.

For many years thereafter he used to touch me on my chest or back, over my heart, lightly, while parting or meeting, and the tension fell away from me like sand in the sun.

•

I met him the same evening at a large dinner party at my aunt's house on Warden Road. He crossed the room, sat beside me, and asked, "What books do you read?"

"Comics and magazines," I replied. He asked me to get a pencil and paper and told me to write down the names of authors: Aldous Huxley, D. H. Lawrence, P. G. Wodehouse, Lewis Mumford, Sinclair Lewis, Emil Ludwig, "especially Napoleon," and Bertrand Russell, among others. He said I should read books written by these writers.

"Have you read them?" I asked.

"No," he replied, "but my brother did."

•

Until I was sixteen I was innocent of sex. After that it became a half-understood ecstasy. I went to see Krishnaji in Benares that winter. I traveled in a third-class train compartment across India with Rao Sahab Patwardhan—it took twenty-four hours, and we shared the compartment with local milkmen, cows, vegetable vendors, and other villagers. Though I stayed in Rajghat, on the banks of the Ganges, where schools and a college had been started decades ago by Krishnaji, and where everyone including Krishnaji stayed, I did not meet him for two days.

And then one evening I saw Krishnaji from a distance on his daily walk. He came up to me, asked how I was, and continued walking. I did not see him again for two days. I was extremely depressed and lonely. I cried alot. Suddenly the desire to understand sex became very strong. The next day I went to talk to Krishnaji about it.

"Thought is the sexual problem," he said. "Listen to desire as you would to a song, or to the breeze amongst the trees."

He said, "Don't let sex precipitate you into marriage. If you marry a girl who is not beautiful you won't be happy. You will play around with others."

"And if I married someone very beautiful?"

"Oh no, that won't make you happy—she will play around."

•

After that, at Rajghat, we went for a walk every day. We walked by the river, the Ganga, and through mango groves. We used to take the old road to Sarnath, and he told me, "The Buddha walked here."

Then he said, "It is very important to do something you really love. I know a man who loves painting, and he paints. His relatives look after him. Once you take a job, or anything like that, then the struggle begins, of wanting a better position, ambition, outdoing your colleagues, competition. It will wear you out, destroy you.

He continued, "Do what you love. You will notice, while playing tennis, that if you play because you enjoy it rather than with the thought of winning, you will play much better.

"I used to be a scratch golfer," he added, "but I could not play if there was a tournament or a wager on the game."

We walked silently for a while, and then he said, "At your age you can do anything you want, in three months, if you set your mind to it."

•

I was sitting with Krishnaji in his room overlooking the river. We sat in silence, and then he said, "I wish you could travel with me, and meet the variety of people I see. Doctors, writers, scientists, artists, so-called religious men, philosophers, wives and mothers and husbands, clerks, bureaucrats, and their bosses…"

"Yes, I'd like to travel with you," I replied.

"One day you will, you will see," he said.

He then asked me, "When you read certain authors, do you feel the urge to write?"

"Yes," I replied.

He suggested that I should write, that it would bring order and clarity. He told me that even when he was ill and tired, he used to write for half an hour every day. Sometimes he used to force himself to do it, though he admitted he should not have done that.

"Writing will help you in everyday life, in mathematics, in conversation. The most important thing is that when you are mature you have the capacity to see a thing to its very end. The mind becomes sharp and clear through writing, discussing."

Then he added, "Write every day. A few pages, get a loose-leaf notebook, but write every day."

He said, "I write between interviews, on planes, a few pages every day. It is part of your life, not separate from it."

And so I started a diary. I quote from the entry dated 20 March 1957: "…somehow, after my talk with Krishnaji in Benares, I am no longer troubled by sexual thoughts."

I was almost eighteen years old.

•

I went to London, to study, at nineteen. The next year Krishnaji came and invited me to Mrs. Bindley's apartment in Kensington. He asked me a great many questions about my London life and then took me upstairs and opened a cupboard. Inside was a row of suits—from Savile Row.

He said, "Take them, take whatever you want."

I took my jacket off, and even I could smell my unbathed body. He tried to help me put on his jackets, but they were too tight, and after some time he said, "No, they won't fit." He gave me his ties and electric shaver and said, "I wish I could take you to Huntsman and outfit you with suits and then to Lobb's for shoes."

He added, "Be scrupulously clean. And you must be well dressed. Always, even at home when you are alone."

•

Fear of madness surfaced and panicked me when I was twenty-two. My father had had fits. He left my mother when I was six or seven, and I didn't see him again till I was nineteen, just before I left for England. He was educated at Balliol College, Oxford, and entered the Indian Civil Service, and then he had given it all up, including a good job in a business organization, to teach engineering at a university.

My father told me two things. He said, "I want you to know that my mental instability is not hereditary. You have nothing to fear. Secondly, it is not the result of any degeneration or dissipation. It's a question of biochemical balances in the body."

(Later, much later, I used to wonder whether the lithium in the blood was not more important than iron in the soul.)

Three years after my father told me I had nothing to fear, I was engulfed by the fear of madness. I was on a short holiday in Bombay, in August 1961. I became engaged to the girl I had known for six years and was generally happy when this fear came curving into my consciousness.

Krishnaji was in Paris. I was due to return to London in September. I wrote to him, and he welcomed me in his rooms in an apartment on the Left Bank near the Seine. His host was Carlo Suares and a friend, Léon De Vidas, was with him. He took me aside, listened to me carefully, and asked, "Do you exercise?"

The next day he told me, "Don't worry, you won't go mad."

The fear of madness has never returned.

Krishnamurti arranged for Monsieur De Vidas to invite me to stay with him for a few days in his house in the valley of the Dordogne.

I went to Tournon-d'Agenais, saw the frescoes of Lascaux, was a vegetarian in the heart of France, and in such close proximity to the great chateaus of Bordeaux and the Cognac district I didn't drink.

The fear of madness has never returned.

•

For over a decade thereafter I did not meet Krishnaji. I married, spent several years in Europe, and returned to India, all innocence gone.

The unintentional birth of my first child was a shock ("She comes into being as I anoint you with kisses"). I took a job.

I was in my thirties when I met Krishnaji again. He stayed at Sterling Apartments, where I lived in Bombay, and I used to walk with him every day on the racecourse. One evening, driving him back to the apartment, I started asking him about beauty and the relationship between men and women (we were alone in the car).

"When I was young," he said, "I lived in Paris for many months at a time. My brother was with me. I was well dressed, and I liked walking in the streets of Paris and going to good restaurants. And do you know, not one woman approached me or looked at me suggestively."

"I didn't know you went to restaurants," I said.

"Oh, occasionally," he replied. "My brother and I would engage in a long conversation with the headwaiter, in French of course, and order good wine. We then made some excuse about not feeling too well and ordered only vegetarian food. We gave the wine to the waiter."

And then he told me about a legendary Hollywood film star. He said they were in a house in Southern California, and she was with a world-famous musician.

"When she saw me, she stopped talking to him and embraced me, and later I went down to see her to her car, she put her arms around me again. I was taken aback, and she could see it."

On the plane from London to Los Angeles, Krishnamurti points out a mountain of ice that casts the shadow of a cathedral.

"Was she very beautiful?" I asked.

"No matter how beautiful..." he answered.

●

Many years later he said to me, "I am not against sex, it's natural when people are young. But now, Asit, see if you can look at sex differently."

"What do you mean by that?" I asked.

He said, "Don't suppress it. But don't give in to it. And don't run away from it."

"Then what do I do, if I don't suppress it, not turn away from it, nor give in to it?" I asked.

"Try it," he said, "you will see."

I did. I felt the most astonishing energy, a feeling of being totally alive. He said he could see the change in me. He left soon afterward for London. The feeling lasted a week, and I have never been able to recapture it.

●

We are in England in February. Krishnamurti and I are staying at Brockwood Park, the KFE school in Hampshire.

Krishnaji is wearing a beret. It is cold outside, but he does not miss his walk. We return to the school and stand in the principal's office, where there is a huge picture of Krishnamurti taken in 1929. I photograph Krishnamurti in his beret standing next to his photograph. Krishnamurti is talking on the phone. He has never been good at it, and the conversation is brief.

The next day we take a direct flight to Los Angeles. This is the polar route, and there are vistas of whiteness. "No landmarks," I remark to Krishnaji, who is writing.

"Wait," he remarks. "In a few minutes, to your right, you will see an ice formation that casts a shadow like a cathedral."

The hostess, overhearing the conversation, says, "There are no landmarks or icebergs here."

"Wait," Krishnamurti persists. "You will see."

I load my camera and look out the window—just in time. Below us is a mountain of ice, and its shadow is that of a cathedral. I take some pictures as it recedes and look in wonder at Krishnaji. He has gone back to writing.

●

"When you have no psychological memory," he said, "your memory of physical things will be excellent. You know, I once spent a week blindfolded, I wanted to experiment, to find out what would happen. Of course, the other senses became much sharper."

●

Krishnaji and I were walking on the road leading out of the school at Rishi Valley. Krishnaji had turned to look at Rishi Konda, the hill that gives the valley its name. The sun had turned the sky red, miraculous as water becoming wine.

"That is what you must salute," he said.

Krishnaji looked and said once again, with hands folded and held high above and in front of his head, "That is what one salutes."

"Do you know," he said, "when I first saw the Parthenon, I fell to my knees...thank God nobody else was there."

We walked silently, and on returning stood outside the open assembly hall, where a great Indian singer was singing.

Krishnamurti stood in the darkness for some time, listening, and then went forward and sat quickly on the floor, where people had left their shoes and slippers. The audience inside was enraptured, and no one noticed Krishnamurti sitting quietly and listening to the singer singing to God, calling to him. Krishnaji listened for two hours, and then as he walked back to his room in total darkness, he said, "Do you know, all those songs were devotional, religious. None of the I-love-you-you-love-me nonsense of the West."

The singer continued long past midnight.

•

Krishnaji often asked me about computers and artificial intelligence. He saw it as a threat to the human mind; if the muscles of the mind were not exercised, the brain would deteriorate.

"Do you think that they will create a computer like the human mind?" he asked.

I replied, "The Japanese are attempting it, their so-called Fifth Generation Computer. They don't know what intelligence is, and that is the problem they are tackling. If they can find out what intelligence is, they feel they can create a machine to emulate human intelligence, to simulate thinking."

Krishnaji said, "So they are approaching intelligence through thought, thinking?"

"Yes," I said.

"Then it is totally wrong. Thought has nothing to do with intelligence, can never lead to it.

"And yet," he added, "people don't see the great challenge to the human mind, to consciousness, of the computer and genetic engineering and the new technologies. Shall we have a discussion, sir?"

And so we had many discussions, in many places, with many people, but that is in another entry, and besides the dialogue is not dead.

•

"If I knew the Buddha would be speaking here tomorrow, nothing in the world could stop me from going to listen to him. And I would follow him to the very end," Krishnaji said at lunchtime, in Arya Vihar, at Ojai.

A famous physicist from London and a well-known New York psychologist were present. There had evidently been discussion for many days about the validity of psychoanalysis. Krishnamurti said, "Analysis cannot lead to understanding or insight—observation and not analysis."

Before lunch the psychologist told Krishnamurti that he had not yet lost their "fight," it was only "the fifth round." Krishnamurti said quietly, "For me there is only one round."

Krishnamurti woke early in the morning, did over an hour of yogic exercises, dressed in a dark blue shirt and blue cardigan, went to the Oak Grove and spoke to three thousand people passionately, for an hour, from 11:30 A.M. to 12:30 P.M., on a beautiful cool day, then to Arya Vihar, lunched, and at the lunch table spoke intensely till 4:00 in the evening, went for a brisk walk for forty-five minutes at 5:00, and then returned to Pine Cottage.

It was Krishnamurti's eighty-fifth birthday.

•

We had just returned from a walk through the Grove, on the grounds of Brockwood Park, in England. It was the end of May,

and the woods were in blossom, the tall trees with flowers at their feet.

"Have you not noticed, sir," he said, "that when you enter a forest, the first time there is a strange atmosphere, as if nature, the trees, do not want you to enter. You hesitate, and say, 'It's alright,' and walk in quietly. The second day the resistance is less. And the third day it is gone."

I do not communicate with nature, and so this was something I had never discussed with Krishnamurti.

He said that he was doing his asanas in a small room in a cottage in India when he noticed a monkey watching him. "There were bars on the window, and the monkey stretched out his hand through the bars. I held his hand. It was the most extraordinary hand I have felt, rough on the palm, and very soft and silken on top. I held the monkey's hand for a few minutes, and then I saw that the monkey wanted to come in. I said, 'You can't come in. There is no room'. And after a while, still holding the monkey's hand, I said I had to continue my exercises, and the monkey went away."

He then told me stories about his encounters with animals—tigers and bears and rattlesnakes and even a lynx.

He said, "If you are sensitive, you are sensitive to everything. I cannot cut a rose, or any flower while it is alive. Do you look at flowers, trees, really look?"

"No," I replied.

"You miss a great deal if you don't," he continued. "One day I was walking in Benares, and we passed a grove of mango trees. My companion said that the trees hadn't borne fruit for many years, and they were to be cut down. 'Watch out!' I said to the trees. 'If you don't bear fruit you will be cut down!'"

"And what happened?" I asked.

"They bore fruit that year," he replied. "I am not saying it had anything to do with me."

•

Krishnaji and I left for London from Brockwood Park. Krishnamurti to a dentist—his tooth had been giving pain—and I on my way back to Bombay.

Krishnamurti came down the staircase at 9:45 A.M., looking extremely elegant.

The weather was good, the sun out, no clouds or signs of rain. I photographed Krishnamurti talking to Brockwood Park students at Petersfield station. We got a compartment to ourselves. Then Krishnamurti asked me to sit opposite him and said, leaning forward, "Is your brain alright?"

I was a little puzzled by the question. He then asked, "Is your brain free of conflict?"

I said, "No."

He said, "You know, any strong emotion is a shock to the brain. Anger, sudden anger, fear, a feeling of anxiety, all these upset the brain, and the brain gets affected."

I asked, "What about positive emotions?"

He said, "Like what?"

"Joy," I replied, "or ecstasy."

Krishnamurti smiled. "Oh, that happens rarely, doesn't it?"

He continued, "You must rest your brain between meetings, between appointments. When you are going to the office, on the way, look around you, don't keep thinking of what you are going to do or say at meetings. If you do, you have already formed a pattern, an expectation, based on your past experience of the person or the situation. That is the worst thing that can happen to the brain, constantly forming patterns, going round in grooves, thinking all the time. When I go to give a talk, my mind has no thought in it, so when I speak all the energy and alertness is there.

"You must exercise, and eat properly, and keep the brain healthy and functioning," Krishnamurti said, "otherwise it gets you later on. How old are you? Almost forty-one? That's not young."

●

As I grew older the effect his words had on me lasted for a shorter period. He used to watch me eat, and drink, and put on weight. He told me, "Be careful, sir. Your heart and your brain. Become slender and vital. Skip every seventh meal. Fill a tub with ice-cold water and take hip baths." He showed me stomach exercises, asked me to do them every day. His own stomach, which I touched, was hard and hollow. He told me his weight, at 51 kg., hadn't changed since his youth and that's why he could wear suits that were fifty years old. He taught me breathing exercises.

"Become slim and elegant," he said as he gave me his shirts and ties.

I talked to him about my frustrations, and how I would eat and drink through boredom and loneliness.

He told me, "If I had a wife, children, a job, I would still have two hours of leisure. And in those two hours I would go into fear, sorrow, desire, the process of thought. I would work at it, give it everything I've got, those hours would become my whole life."

He said, "You must have a certain amount of money. How much money do you need? Do you have it? If not, work for it, do your business really well, and make the money you need." I was quiet.

"Where would you like to live?" he asked. "What about California? Or India? If I did not have to live the way I do, I would live quietly in a village in India, such as Rishi Valley.

"The world is becoming a very dangerous place," he added, "what are you going to do? And you have children...."

"What would you do if you had children?" I asked.

"First of all," he continued, "think of them and not of yourself. Their lives and not yours. And don't use the word 'my' when you refer to them."

He talked about not being able to see something clearly if you are too close to it, a book becomes illegible if you hold it too close.

"If there is affection, you create an atmosphere where they feel secure, at home. I would talk to them about that. And then I would be silent with them, show them what it is to be quiet, silent. In that silence, their senses awaken, so that they look at a tree, listen to a bird, smell a flower."

"I would give them a good education, not spoil them," he continued. "Sir, there is no security. There is no protection. What can you do?"

And then he talked about protection. There are various occult societies, he said, and various practices. In some societies, at one stage you are initiated as a disciple to a master, and he makes an image of you, and every emotion, thought, and action of yours is reflected in that image, so that the master can watch over you. And at another stage two beings (he called them angels) are supposed to protect you.

"If you draw upon that power, however, it becomes weaker."

And then he added, "You must not do anything that is dangerous. You have to be very careful about this sort of thing."

"Why?" I asked.

"When one is protected, one has to be very watchful, for the bad as well as the good will be exaggerated," he answered.

As he said this he was very serious and a strange atmosphere filled the room.

He asked, "Can you feel it? If you talk about it you attract it..."

Then he got up and asked me to sit on a straight-backed chair. He walked a short distance, looked out of the window, jerked his hands as if shaking something off, and then came and stood behind me and with indescribable gentleness he placed his hands on my eyes, and then slowly drew his fingers over my head toward him. He did this several times, stopping occasionally to touch the spot between the eyes and at the top and back of the head and then the heart and finally, quietly, he laid his hands on my shoulders. As he walked away he said, "Sit quietly for a few minutes."

●

"You must never let anyone have power over you," he once told me, "and you must not have power over anyone else.

"When I left the Theosophical Society, and all the wealth and comfort surrounding me, Mrs. Besant said, 'What will happen to you? How will you live? How will you survive?'

"You understand, I had not been educated or trained for any profession. But here I am fifty years later...sometimes I wonder what I have done to deserve all this...

"Do the right thing, and the right things will happen to you," he said finally.

●

We were in Sterling Apartments in Bombay. He had noticed my lethargy and had taken me aside to talk to me.

"Do you love your children?" he asked. "Do you love anything? Do you love me?"

"Do you think I take you for granted?" I asked.

"Maybe that is it," he said. "Why don't you write to me, every day? You will see the difference it makes."

And then after a while he said, "If you spent some time with me I could change your life."

We were silent, and then he went in to have a bath. When he came out, just before lunch, he said to me, "I apologize for saying that."

"For saying what, sir?" I asked.

"That I could change your life."

•

Krishnaji ends a discourse to six thousand people in Bombay, and the energy that wells up in him during his talks is still emanating. The crowds surge around him. A policeman calls on them to move. Krishnamurti stops him by a sign and takes his hand and holds it. The policeman flings aside his baton and prostrates himself at Krishnamurti's feet. Krishnamurti lifts him up and, still holding his hand, enters the car. As the car moves, the policeman runs with it, refusing to let go of the hand.

We return and sit at the dinner table at Sterling Apartments.

"Why are you wasting your life?" he asks.

There is complete silence. He looks at me and says, "If you do not answer that question the moment it is asked, then you are wasting your life."

"And if I do answer immediately?"

"Oh, then you are an aristocrat."

•

He asked me, "Are you afraid of death?"

"I suppose so," I replied, "though at the moment there is no fear."

We had been talking about Yukio Mishima's commentary on *Hagakure*, a centuries'-old manual written for Samurais. I told Krishnaji that the book talked about always being ready for death, every morning to prepare for it. And that it was very important to be well dressed and even use makeup if necessary so that death would find one with rosy cheeks. To live with death all the time. And the Italians have a saying: "May death find you fully alive."

"Sir," I said, "twenty years ago I heard you say that one must enter the house of death with all one's senses fully alert, not when one is old and decrepit..."

"Yes," he replied. "For me the line dividing life and death has always been very thin. It would be so easy to live to be 150, but the body wears out with constant traveling and crowded airports and smoke-filled rooms, and so perhaps I shall live for another ten or fifteen years."

"What would happen if you were told that you were going to die tomorrow morning?" I asked.

He said, "Nothing. I would live exactly as before. The thought that death was so imminent wouldn't enter my mind again, and nothing would change."

•

Last summer I went to Switzerland to see Krishnamurti. We were sitting quietly together in Saanen. Krishnamurti was in his bathrobe, sitting straight on his bed, while I sat on a chair at the foot of the bed. Through the window you could see the snow on a high mountain, and nearer were the half-crescents of two other mountains, their points meeting to create the valley.

We had conversed for an hour or so, on bringing up children, education, meditation, death. It was a fragile conversation, touching profound matters lightly.

Suddenly he said, "If I were asked whether I had wasted my life, whether I am wasting it now, I would answer 'I do not know.'"

He was silent, and then he said, "I don't think so," and finally he added, "No."

"I might be wrong," he hesitated, and then said, "I ask nothing of the world. Perhaps that is the answer. I want nothing, from human beings or the Gods. Nothing, from anyone. If death came just now and said, 'You go this evening,' it would be alright."

He smiled. "You see, it's the same thing. I want nothing from this world or any other, and so I would go with death."

That evening I repeated the conversation as we sat in the car, before the walk through the woods above the stream in Gstaad.

"When I hear that it brings tears to my eyes."

And I remembered the Buddha, who said, "I obtained not the least thing from complete unexcelled awakening, and that is why it is complete unexcelled awakening."

•

POSTSCRIPT

I meet Krishnaji every year. Sometimes in Ojai, or New York, Saanen and Brockwood, and in Delhi, Rishi Valley, Madras, and Bombay. We go for walks and have long discussions in small groups, and sometimes just with each other. He stays in our apartment on his visits to Bombay.

As I write this I am forty-five years old. Krishnaji, in his ninetieth year, is twice my age. I finish writing and read a poem, Walt Whitman's *Leaves of Grass*:

> *...Who wishes to walk with me?*
>
> *Will you speak before I am gone?*
> *Will you prove already too late?*

And then a little later,

> *...You will hardly know who I am or what I mean,*
> *But I shall be good health to you nevertheless,*
> *And filter and fibre your blood.*
>
> *Failing to fetch me at first keep encouraged,*
> *Missing me one place search another,*
> *I stop some where waiting for you.*

INDIA

Krishnamurti in India at eighty-five.

Krishnamurti stays here in the corner room on the upper floor when he visits the school he founded in 1926 in Rishi Valley.

Rishi Valley is approximately twenty kilometers from Madanapalle, where Krishnamurti was born. Rishi means "sage." According to legend, for centuries rishis came to this valley to live, in meditation and the search for God.

Krishnamurti in his room writing letters and consulting a dictionary.

Above: Krishnamurti prepares for his daily walk.
Right: After a talk with students, Krishnamurti puts on his sandals to walk back to his room.

Krishnamurti walks for as much as five kilometers—regardless of the weather. There is very little conversation. He has said that not a single thought touches his mind during these walks.

Krishnamurti walks on the grounds of the school with the late Mrs. Gandhi. The immense banyan tree in the background drew him to the site where he established the Rishi Valley School.

During the day Krishnamurti walks with an umbrella to protect him against the sun.
Below: Walking with Narayan, the principal of the school.

Krishnamurti points to a star at dusk.

Above and opposite: Krishnamurti addresses students in the school's assembly hall.

Following: Krishnamurti speaks simply, articulately—his hands and face are vital yet gentle in their gestures.

Above: After his talk to the students, he answers their questions.
Opposite: Krishnamurti sits in on musical programs and school plays.

Left: Krishnamurti meets with teachers at the school *(above)* and some members of his three foundations *(below)*.
Above: Krishnamurti with Nandini Mehta, Mary Zimbalist, Pama Patwardhan, and Pupul Jayakar.

Krishnamurti with Radha Burnier, president of the Theosophical Society.

Krishnamurti with Achuyt Patwardhan, one of his closest associates in India.

Above: Discussions with friends and associates take place at lunch. Facing the table are Krishnamurti, Alan Hooker, Mary Cadogan, and Dorothy Simmons. *Below:* Krishnamurti chanting Sanskrit verses with Narayan and Sunanda Patwardhan in Bombay.

In Madras, Krishnamurti stays in Vasant Vihar,
headquarters of the Krishnamurti Foundation of India (KFI).

Left: Walking on the beach at Adyar, where he was "discovered" in 1909. He was fourteen years old then, one among many, like the young boys playing in the background below.
Above: Krishnamurti walks with Rimpoche, a Tibetan monk.

Above: At a public talk in India.
On the podium, the silence of his presence creates order, no matter how large the crowd.
Opposite: As admirers press around after his talk, Krishnamurti reaches out and touches those who come to greet him.

The hands of Krishnamurti.

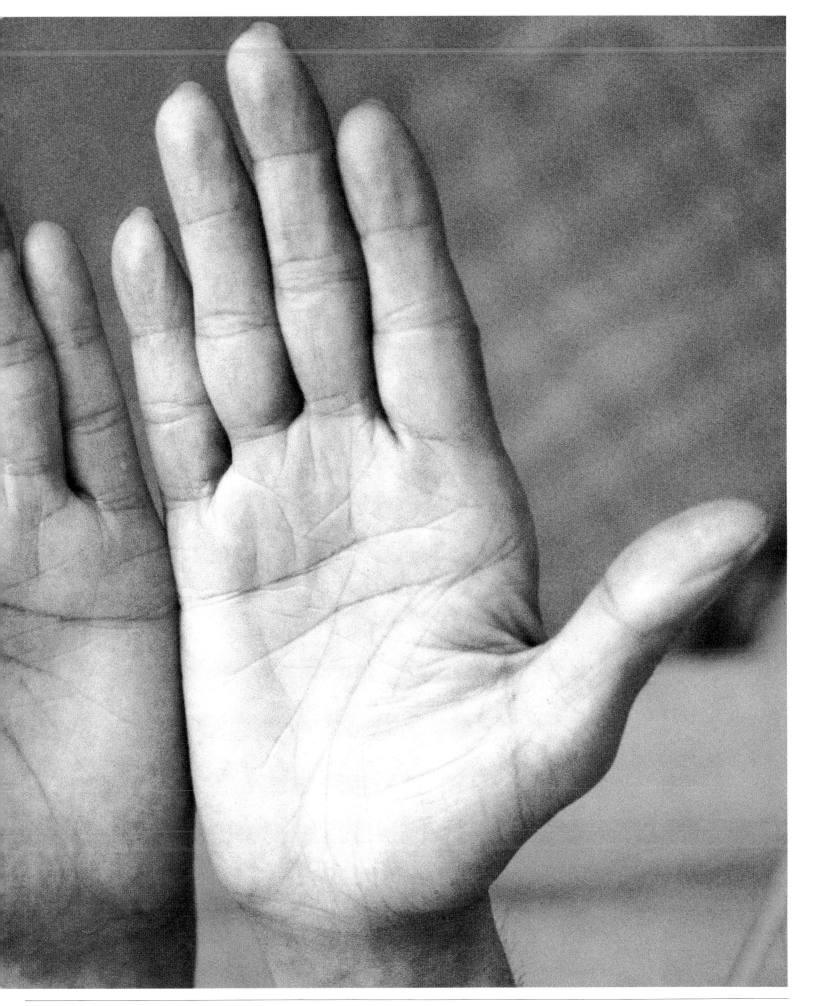

Left: Krishnamurti pauses during a discussion.
Above: Listening to Beethoven's Ninth Symphony after a public talk in Bombay.

CALIFORNIA

Krishnamurti at a public address in California. It is his eighty-fifth birthday.

The pepper tree at Pine Cottage, Ojai, California. Krishnamurti underwent his first "experiences" under this tree in 1922.

Krishnamurti has stayed here, at Pine Cottage, since 1922. Pine Cottage sits in the Ojai Valley.
At his school in Ojai, Krishnamurti talks to parents and staff about education and the significance of life.

Krishnamurti in the new addition to Pine Cottage.

Krishnamurti helps to prepare breakfast with Mary Zimbalist.
In the West, he helps clear the table, wash the dishes, clean the kitchen.

Mary Zimbalist and Erna and Theo Lilliefelt join Krishnamurti for breakfast at Pine Cottage.

In his room at Pine Cottage.

Krishnamurti breakfasts alone in bed.

Krishnamurti prepares for a walk he will take in the hills surrounding the valley.

Left: On his walk with Mary Zimbalist and Theo Lilliefelt, Krishnamurti meets a jogger who offers him bee pollen. Krishnamurti is delighted. *Above and below:* Climbing over rocks in the valley.

Krishnamurti walks to Arya Vihar from Pine Cottage.

Krishnamurti lunches at Arya Vihar.
The cook, Michael Krohnen *(right)*, tells Krishnamurti the news of the world every day.

Krishnamurti always lets others precede him.

Krishnamurti loves to garden and does so energetically.

Krishnamurti and Mary Zimbalist at the Santa Barbara airport, where they have come to pick up a friend.

Above: A crowd assembles to hear Krishnamurti speak at the Oak Grove.
Right: On the podium before Krishnamurti's talk commences, Alan Kishbaugh attaches a microphone to him.
It is May 11, 1980. On this day Krishnamurti is eighty-five years old.

As he sits in silence on the platform, Krishnamurti's presence reaches out and draws his listeners close to him. Then he starts to speak.

Returning to Arya Vihar after his talk.

ENGLAND

Krishnamurti on the grounds of his school at Brockwood Park.

The Krishnamurti Foundation of England (KFE) school of Brockwood Park, Hampshire, England.
The Brockwood Park School was founded in 1969 with money a donor had originally intended for Krishnamurti's
personal use. "You are seventy years old," the donor had said to Krishnamurti, "I'll buy you a house in the
south of France, provide you with a cook, a maid, a car, and so on. You can stay there the rest of your life."
"I'm not interested," Krishnamurti replied. "If you really mean to donate this money, could we use it to start a school?"

Above: Walking with Dorothy Simmons, principal of the school.
Right: Krishnamurti in the principal's office with Doris Pratt, standing next to a portrait of his taken in 1929.

Most people half his age cannot keep up with him—here, near Brockwood Park.

Krishnamurti lunches with Mary Lutyens, a close friend he has known for seventy-five years and whose family looked after him while he was a young man living in England. Lutyens' father was the architect of New Delhi, her grandfather a viceroy of India, while she herself has written a two-volume biography on the life of Krishnamurti.

Krishnamurti and Dr. David Böhm, a physicist, friend, and associate, during a discussion at Brockwood Park.

Above and opposite bottom: After a talk, Krishnamurti returns to a tent where lunch is served and he mixes with the audience.
Opposite top: The crowd gathers for his talk.

Krishnamurti bidding goodbye to the students and faculty as he prepares to leave Brockwood Park for California.

Krishnamurti chats with students from the school as they all wait for the train to London.

On the train to London.

Above and opposite: On a plane from London. Krishnamurti reads, writes, watches a movie, eats, sleeps, and takes his walk up and down the aisle of the plane on a long flight.
Below: Krishnamurti looks at thrillers and other light reading before catching his flight.

SWITZERLAND

Krishnamurti in front of Chalet Tannegg in Gstaad.

Gstaad, Switzerland. Krishnamurti has been coming here since 1959.
During his stay each year, he gives public talks in Saanen, four miles away.

In Gstaad, Krishnamurti stays at Chalet Tannegg, a rented chalet.

Krishnamurti's stride is long and vigorous.
Here he walks in the woods above a stream, his favorite place for a walk in Gstaad.

Krishnamurti writing, after his morning exercises.

In his room, Krishnamurti reads a letter before lunch.

Krishnamurti with Alain Naudé, Minakshi Chandmal, Mary Zimbalist, and Dr. Parchure.

Krishnamurti helps carry visitors' luggage outside the chalet.

Krishnamurti on the balcony at Chalet Tannegg.